World Cities

MOSCOW

Christine Hatt

Belitha Press

First published in the UK in 1999 by

 Belitha Press Limited
London House, Great Eastern Wharf,
Parkgate Road, London SW11 4NQ

ISBN 1 84138 016 4

British Library Cataloguing in Publication Data for this
book is available from the British Library.

Printed in Singapore

Editor Stephanie Bellwood
Designer Hayley Cove
Map illustrator Lorraine Harrison
Picture researcher Kathy Lockley
Consultant Elizabeth Lewis

Picture acknowledgements
AA Photo Library: 15bl, 18b, 32b.
AKG London: 40t, /Tretyakov Gallery, Moscow 9t, 36t.
Associated Press Picture Library: 21b, 25b, 42-3b.
Bridgeman Art Library London/New York: /Private Collection/Novosti
    10t, 18t, /Tretyakov Gallery, Moscow 32t, 36b, 40b.
Jean-Loup Charmet: 9b.
Eye Ubiquitous/Featurescapes 26b, /Gary Trotter 12b, /James Davis Travel
    Photography 5cr, 28t, 29b, 29t, 31t.
Robert Harding Picture Library: 4, 13b, 15rc, 20b, 22, 24b, 28b, 34t, 37b.
David King Collection: 24t.
Novosti (London): cover, title page, 5bl, 8b, 8t, 10b, 11b, 11t, 14, 19l, 20t,
    23t, 25t, 27t, 31b, 33t, 35b, 38t, 39t, 39b, 41c, 43b.
Rex Features: cover, 12t, 21t, 23rc, 26t, 27b, 38b, 41b.
TRIP: 13t, 15tl, 16, 17tl, 17bl, 17tr, 19r, 23bl, 30b, 30t, 33b, 34b, 35t, 37t,
    41t, 42t, 43t.

Words in **bold** are explained in the glossary on pages 46 and 47.

CONTENTS

Moscow is the capital and largest city of the world's largest country – Russia. This vast nation extends for 9,000 kilometres across two continents, from

Europe in the west to Asia in the east. Moscow is on the flat plain of European Russia and covers 994 square kilometres. Its population of almost nine million makes it Europe's largest city, and the sixth largest in the world as a whole. The map on the left shows the city of Moscow as well as the Moscow region (in yellow).

Circular layout

The city of Moscow, known in Russian as *Moskva*, began as a small settlement on the banks of the Moskva River and gradually expanded. At its heart are the Kremlin, a huge, walled enclosure containing many magnificent buildings, and the wide open spaces of Red Square. Beyond this central area, highways and railways divide the city into five great circles, linked by smaller roads.

The Kremlin's walls, ▲ towers and buildings are in the foreground of this Moscow view. In the distance are the high-rise blocks where many ordinary Muscovites live.

FAST FACTS
MOSCOW

STATUS
Capital of Russia and of the Moscow region

AREA
994 square kilometres

POPULATION
8,650,000 (1997)

GOVERNING BODY
Council led by a mayor

CLIMATE
Temperatures average 19 to 36°C in August
and -13 to -29°C in February

TIME ZONE
Greenwich Mean Time plus 3 hours

CURRENCY
1 rouble = 100 kopeks

OFFICIAL LANGUAGE
Russian, written in the **Cyrillic alphabet**

Federal city

The official name of Russia is the Russian Federation, because it has a **federal** form of government. This means that each of its 89 **republics**, regions and other political units has its own government, and also takes part in the national government. Moscow is one of only two cities among the 89 members.

Moscow government

Moscow has a council with as much power as the government of a republic. The city is divided into 10 districts, and each elects its own council members. The whole city votes for a mayor, who is the leader of Moscow's government.

◄ The marble-covered Beliy Dom (White House), where the Russian parliament meets regularly.

Capital city

As Moscow is Russia's capital, it is the place where the national government is based. It is also capital of the 47,000-square-kilometre Moscow region (see map), so the regional governor and administration are housed there.

◄ Yury Luzhkov, Moscow's mayor (right) talks with President Boris Yeltsin at the opening of Moscow's 850th anniversary celebrations (see page 11).

MAP OF THE CITY

This map shows central Moscow as it looks today. Many of the places mentioned in the book are marked. The inset map gives a closer view of the Kremlin and Red Square.

CENTRAL MOSCOW

SADOVOYE (GARDEN) RING

BOULEVARD RING

see inset

MOSKVA RIVER

1. Gorky Park
2. New University
3. Beliy Dom
4. Ministry of Foreign Affairs
5. Chekhov House Museum
6. Gorky House Museum
7. Bolshoi Theatre
8. Old University

9. Pushkin Museum of Fine Arts
10. Cathedral of Christ the Saviour
11. Tretyakov Gallery
12. Andronikov Monastery and
    Rublev Museum
13. Moscow Arts Theatre
14. Lubyanka
15. Moscow Conservatory

16. Leninsky Komsomol Theatre
17. Central Children's Theatre
18. Obraztsov Puppet Theatre
19. Old Circus
20. New Circus
21. St Petersburg Vokzal
22. Sparrow Hills
23. Church of the Great Ascension

THE KREMLIN AND
RED SQUARE

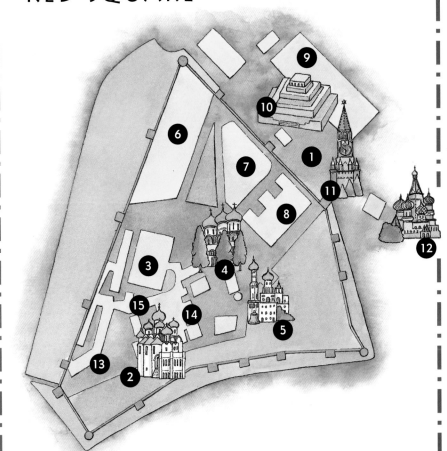

1. Red Square
2. Cathedral of the Annunciation
3. Palace of Congresses
4. Cathedral of the Assumption
5. Ivan the Great Bell Tower
6. Arsenal
7. Senate
8. Presidium

9. GUM
10. Lenin Mausoleum
11. Saviour Tower
12. St Basil's Cathedral
13. Armoury Palace
14. Palace of Facets
15. Terem Palace

7 *Moscow*

The first Russian **state**, known as Kievan Rus, was set up in the 9th century AD. By the 12th century, it was divided into **principalities**. Moscow began as a small settlement in a principality called Suzdal. No-one is quite sure when this was, though the first known record of the name Moscow dates from 1147. In 1156 the ruler of Suzdal, Prince Yury Dolgorukiy, built a wooden fort in Moscow with a wall round it. This was the original Kremlin.

This modern painting ➤ shows the Kremlin and its surrounding wooden wall in the early 14th century.

THE TWO-HEADED EAGLE

The **emblem** of Russia is a two-headed eagle. It dates back many hundreds of years. A single eagle was the symbol of the emperors of Rome. When the **Roman Empire** ended in the 5th century AD, it was followed by the **Byzantine Empire**. This empire lasted until 1453 and adopted a two-headed eagle as its emblem. Moscow had trading links with the Byzantine Empire, and **Tsar** Ivan III later married the niece of the last Byzantine emperor. Ivan III decided to take the two-headed eagle symbol to represent Muscovy. Later it became the emblem of all Russia.

Muscovy

Moscow's position on the Moskva River allowed **merchants** to reach it easily from other rivers, so it grew into an important trading centre. Then in 1237 the **Mongols**, a warlike people from Central Asia, attacked the city and burned it down. The city was rebuilt, but for more than 200 years had to pay **tribute** to the Mongols. In 1263 Moscow became a separate principality called Muscovy, with its own ruler, Prince Daniil. He and his successors expanded Muscovy by conquering other principalities.

Expansion

In 1380 the Russians defeated the Mongols at the Battle of Kulikovo Field. In 1480 Prince Ivan III (Ivan the Great) refused to make any more payments to them and ended their power in Russia. He also made Muscovy the largest state in Europe and extended the Kremlin. Ivan IV (Ivan the Terrible) expanded Muscovy still further during his reign (1533-84).

Tsar Ivan IV earned his ▲ nickname 'the Terrible' by killing thousands of people, including one of his sons.

▲ This 16th-century map shows two rivers in Moscow, the Moskva and the Neglina. Now the Neglina runs underground.

A new capital

Rival tsars fought in Moscow in the early 17th century, then in 1613 the Romanov **dynasty** took over. Peter the Great came to power in 1689 and changed the nation's name from Muscovy to Russia. He felt Moscow was out of touch with modern Europe, so he built the city of St Petersburg on the shores of the Baltic Sea, facing Western Europe. In 1712 this new city became Russia's capital.

Moscow continued to grow and prosper in the 18th century, even though it was no longer Russia's capital. Business people set up many factories there, and the population steadily increased (see page 24). But there were setbacks. Fires raged through the streets in 1737, 1748 and 1752. Then, in 1771, plague struck and more than 57,000 people died.

Russian troops at the Battle of ▲ Borodino. About 70,000 French and Russian soldiers were killed.

Napoleon Bonaparte

In 1812 the French ruler Napoleon Bonaparte invaded Russia. In September the two sides fought the Battle of Borodino near Moscow. Neither side won, but the Russian commander ordered everyone to leave the city. Napoleon's troops moved in to occupy Moscow, but then fire broke out. It burned for six days and destroyed 6,496 houses and 122 churches. The French soon retreated, and the following year the Russians began to rebuild their city.

Revolution

By 1900 Moscow's industry had expanded, but factory workers were poor and badly treated. They began to protest about conditions, and in 1905 **revolution** broke out in St Petersburg and Moscow. It was crushed, but in 1917 the **Russian Revolution** began and a **Communist** government led by Vladimir Lenin took over. In 1918 Moscow became Russia's capital again, and in 1922 Russia was renamed the Union of Soviet Socialist Republics (USSR).

◄ Communist soldiers defended their Moscow headquarters during the Russian Revolution of 1917. Fighting in the city lasted ten days.

Wartime

In June 1941, during the Second World War, German troops invaded the USSR. They came within 30 km of Moscow, but the city was successfully defended. After the war the USSR and other Communist countries opposed Western **capitalist** countries such as the USA and Great Britain, during a period known as the **Cold War**.

▲ Josef Stalin ruled the USSR from 1928 to 1953. He was an ambitious man and ruthlessly killed all opponents (see page 27).

▼ Celebrations marked Moscow's 850th anniversary in 1997. But there are likely to be troubles as well as triumphs ahead.

The Russian Federation

In 1985 Mikhail Gorbachev came to power in the USSR and began to make its government more **democratic**. He also increased contacts with capitalist countries, and in 1990 the Cold War officially ended. In August 1991, Gorbachev's opponents led a **coup** against him. He survived, but the USSR collapsed in December. Russia, the largest and most powerful of its 15 republics, became the Russian Federation, with Moscow as its capital. The new leader, Boris Yeltsin, continued Gorbachev's reforms and in 1993 defeated another coup.

THE PEOPLE OF MOSCOW

People of about 100 different nationalities live in Moscow. Most are Russians, but there are also many people from **republics** that were once part of the USSR, particularly the Ukraine, Belorussia and Armenia.

There are also many Tatars, descendants of the **Mongols** who invaded Russia in the 13th century (see page 9). Moscow has a large Jewish community too.

▲ Thousands of Russia's six million Tatars live in Moscow. Most of the rest, like these women, live in the republic of Tatarstan, to the south.

Moscow's rich business ▼ people – and criminals – can afford luxury cars like this stretch Cadillac limousine.

A growing population

Since the Second World War, the number of people in Moscow has risen steadily. In the past 25 years it has grown by more than two million to just under nine million (see page 5). Most of the city's new inhabitants moved there from the countryside in the hope of finding factory, office or shop work. Many have not settled in central Moscow, but in suburbs such as Babushkin, where new industries provide jobs.

Wealth and power

There is a huge division between rich and poor in modern Moscow. Now that there is more economic freedom, a few fortunate businessmen have grown rich. One of these is Boris Berezovsky, a former car dealer turned billionaire tycoon, who controls television and newspaper companies.

Poverty

Economic changes have also meant that prices have risen and the rouble has fallen in value. Most Muscovites now earn low wages or live on small pensions. They struggle to afford food and housing. Many unemployed people have to survive by selling goods such as bread on the streets.

 Moscow's poor display their meagre goods for sale. Most have so little that they do not even put up a stall.

The rise of racism

The collapse of the USSR has had another serious effect on Moscow's people. As republics became independent, they each wanted to rebuild their national identity. Russia tried to do the same, but some people took this too far and became extreme **nationalists**. They believed that only Russian people should be allowed to live in Russia. Many non-Russians in Moscow, especially **Gypsies** and people from former **Soviet** republics such as Georgia and Azerbaijan, now suffer racist attacks. Jews are also targeted, mainly by the organization *Pamyat* (Memory).

WESTERNIZATION

Many Muscovites are adopting aspects of Western European and American culture. Those with enough money can eat in Pizza Hut or McDonalds, and buy Adidas sportswear or American-style jeans (right). They can even watch English-language films and bands. Young people in particular are making the most of these new opportunities, but many older people are clinging to their traditional ways of life.

Moscow's earliest buildings were made of wood. In the 13th century Prince Daniil (see page 9) ordered the construction of the city's first stone buildings. Since then, magnificent structures in a wide variety of styles have grown up in Russia's capital. But many of the greatest and oldest buildings still stand in the heart of the city – the Kremlin and Red Square.

When St Basil's Cathedral ➤ was completed in 1560, it was all white with gold 'onion' domes. In the 17th century it was painted to create the multi-coloured building that exists today.

The Kremlin

In 1367, after several disastrous fires, the original wooden walls of the Kremlin were replaced with dazzling white limestone. Ivan III (see page 9) demolished all this to make way for red brick walls and towers encircling 28 hectares of land. He also employed Russian and Italian architects to build splendid structures inside the walls. These included the Cathedral of the Assumption, which was used for coronations, and the Cathedral of the Annunciation (right), the private church of the **tsars**.

The Bell Tower

Another important Kremlin landmark is the Ivan the Great Bell Tower. This gold-domed structure was begun in 1505, and reached its present height of 81m in 1600. It contains 21 bells, which were rung to warn Muscovites of approaching enemies. The Assumption Bell weighs 65 tonnes and was tolled three times when a tsar died.

Red Square

Red Square runs along the Kremlin's east wall. In the 15th century it was a marketplace known as the Burnt-Out Site, because fire had once destroyed the area. But by the 17th century attractive buildings stood there, so people called it *Krasnaya* (Beautiful) Square. It is now known as Red Square, because *krasnaya* no longer means 'beautiful' but 'red'. The square is packed with famous landmarks. Among the best known is St Basil's Cathedral, which was built for Ivan the Terrible. It is now a museum.

▲ Lenin's Mausoleum in Red Square was built in 1930. It contains the **embalmed** body of Vladimir Lenin (see page 10).

This stunning building is the Cathedral ▼ of the Annunciation. Its nine domes were covered in gold on the orders of Ivan IV.

STALINIST ARCHITECTURE

Josef Stalin (see page 11) wanted to make Moscow the ideal **Communist** capital, so he set up a committee to decide how to do this. As a result of the committee's plans, seven skyscrapers were built. These included the 172m-high Ministry of Foreign Affairs (above) and the 240m-high Moscow University, the tallest skyscraper in the city (see pages 20-21). The skyscrapers are sometimes known as wedding cake palaces.

OPEN SPACES

To escape from the hustle and bustle of city life, many Muscovites head for the green areas beyond the city border. Here, in a zone covering about 1800 sq km, are oak, pine, fir and birch woods, grassy meadows and winding streams. Moscow itself also has parks and gardens where citizens can rest and play.

Gorky Park

Gorky Park is on the right bank of the Moskva River, just outside the Sadovoye (Garden) Ring. The park covers 242 hectares and was founded in 1928 as the first **Communist** Park of Culture and Rest. Russians who visited it had to listen to political speeches too. Loudspeakers boomed across the park from the government buildings in the Kremlin.

◄ A ferris wheel towers over one of Gorky Park's lakes. The park is named after the Russian writer Maxim Gorky.

The modern park

Today, Gorky Park is very different. Muscovites young and old flock to its funfairs, boating lakes, open-air theatre and skating rink. Others stroll along the river or admire the ornamental gardens. Thousands of people visit the ice sculptures that are displayed every February.

Izmaylovskiy Park

Moscow's 330-hectare Izmaylovskiy Park (right) lies to the east of the city. The park was named after the Izmaylov family, its original owners. In the 16th century it was bought by the Romanovs, who became Russia's ruling **dynasty** (see page 9). They built a cathedral and other buildings on an island in the park. Today the park has cafés, a playground and sports facilities. It leads into the Izmaylovskiy Forest Park, a huge, wooded area where the **tsars** used to hunt.

MOSCOW ZOOPARK

Moscow Zoopark is in the west of the city. It was established in 1864 and taken over by the government in 1919. Today the zoo contains more than 5,000 animals, such as this llama (left) and attracts well over one million visitors every year. Many of the animals live in cramped and unsuitable conditions, and the mayor of Moscow, Yury Luzhkov, has ordered new buildings to be constructed for them.

A flower bed in Moscow's ▼ Botanical Gardens, where weeds threaten to crowd out the roses.

The Botanical Gardens

Moscow's 361-hectare Botanical Gardens are north of the city centre. They were founded in 1945 to provide a home for the largest collection of plants in the USSR. Nowadays visitors can marvel at the extraordinary range of specimens on show, including 16,000 varieties of rose.

◄ The Cathedral of the Intercession stands on the Romanovs' island in Izmaylovskiy Park. The cathedral is famous for its tiled exterior.

HOMES AND HOUSING

Early Moscow homes were made of pine and other woods. Carpenters prepared logs in many sizes, and people slotted them together to build anything from a hut to a palace. The logs were numbered to make them easy to assemble, like modern flat-pack furniture.

The Kitai Gorod, east of Red Square, ▲ was Moscow's early trading quarter. Many merchants built wooden homes there, as this 1912 painting shows.

Wood and stone

Muscovites first built with stone in the 13th century (see pages 14-15), but for 500 years this material was used mainly for public buildings, not houses. From 1714 to 1728, Peter the Great banned all use of stone in Moscow as it was needed for St Petersburg.

Homes of the rich

Wealthy people who did not move to the new capital built many grand homes in Moscow during the 18th century. One of the most spectacular was Ostankino, where the palace was made of plaster-covered wood. During the reign of Catherine the Great (1762-96), many stone mansions were constructed in the city for the rich. But when Moscow was rebuilt after its occupation by Napoleon (see page 10), wood was used for most homes. In 1850, half the city's buildings were still made of logs.

◄ Ostankino Palace was owned by Count Nikolai Sheremetev. The count's servants performed plays for his wealthy friends in the palace's beautiful Theatre Hall.

Communist construction

Population growth in the late 19th century led to a serious housing shortage in Moscow. **Tenement** blocks were hurriedly built, but most people still lived in overcrowded conditions.

After 1917 the USSR's **Communist** rulers tried to improve Moscow housing. In the 1950s and '60s tower-block estates such as Novyye Cheryomushki were built around the capital. These were owned by the state and divided into groups of flats, each with shops and other facilities. Further from the city centre, taller blocks were constructed, using **prefabricated** concrete sections. The flats were of poor quality, but they were cheap, as the state paid most of the rent.

BEYOND THE RING

The Moscow Ring Road was made the city's boundary in 1961, but housing developments soon sprang up beyond it. The most important of these is the new town of Zelenograd (below), to the north of the capital. It was founded in 1963 and is now recognized as one of Moscow's 10 administrative districts (see page 5).

◄ Nikita Khrushchev, ruler of the USSR from 1958 to 1964, ordered thousands of apartment blocks to be built in and around Moscow.

Housing today

There is still a serious housing shortage in Moscow. Thousands of people are on waiting lists and will not receive a new home for several years. Even those with a home have to put up with cramped conditions. Children, parents and grandparents often share a single small flat.

Looking ahead

Since the Communist era ended, the government has begun to sell state housing to private owners. It also encourages housing **co-operatives**, whose members club together to build new homes and renovate old blocks of flats. This may help to solve Moscow's housing problems. In the meantime, the city government has introduced a law that will keep rents low until the year 2000.

EDUCATION

Every child in Russia must attend school from the age of six to fourteen. Many begin their education earlier by joining a nursery. Many also continue into higher education at senior school and university. Moscow is full of places of learning for people of every age, teaching all kinds of skills.

◄ Russian children sledge in their nursery playground. Muscovites often begin their education before the official starting age of six.

Moscow University

In 1702 Peter the Great set up two of Moscow's earliest centres of learning, the School of Artillery and the School of Navigation. They no longer exist, but Moscow University, also founded in the 18th century, has survived. The university was established in 1755 by scientist Mikhail Lomonosov, and the original buildings near the Kremlin are still used. Most of the university's 30,000 students now attend classes on a new site in the Sparrow Hills, south-west of the city centre.

Friendship University

Another important institution in Moscow is the Patrice Lumumba People's Friendship University. It was founded in 1960 and provides education for students who come from developing countries in Africa and elsewhere.

Schools for science

Moscow contains many centres for studying science. The most important is the Academy of Sciences of Russia. It was founded in St Petersburg in 1724, but moved to Moscow in 1934. During the **Soviet** era, members of the Academy of Sciences had to make sure that their research supported **Communist** ideas. Now they are more free, but receive much less money from the government, so they still find it hard to carry out research.

Agriculture

Another Moscow science centre is the Timiryazev Agricultural Academy. It was founded in 1865, then in 1923 was named after K A Timiryazev, a botanist who taught there. Students from around the world now learn scientific farming techniques there.

Andrei Sakharov was a leading member of the ▲ Academy of Sciences and fought to free it from Soviet control. He won the Nobel Peace Prize (1975) and the Albert Einstein Peace Prize (1988) for all his human rights work.

◄ The main building of the new Moscow University has 35 storeys. The gold star on the top weighs an amazing 12 tonnes.

MAKING MUSIC

The Moscow Conservatory is the largest music school in Russia and one of the greatest in the world. It was founded in 1866. The famous Russian

composer Pyotr Tchaikovsky taught at the school for 12 years until 1878, which is why it is also known as the Tchaikovsky Conservatory. Every four years, the internationally famous Tchaikovsky Piano Competition is held in the Conservatory's Great Hall. The 1998 winner was Russian Denis Matsuyev (left).

Before the 1917 revolution, most people in Russia were practising **Orthodox Christians**. Many Muslims, Buddhists and Jews also lived in the country. But under **Communist** rule, people were not allowed to practise religion, and many religious buildings were closed or used for other purposes, for example as restaurants. In 1917 Moscow had 848 churches. By 1990 only 78 were still places of worship.

◄ Danilov Monastery is a 13th-century group of religious buildings founded by Prince Daniil (see page 9). A holy well stands in front of the monastery.

Communism and the Church

In the 1980s, Mikhail Gorbachev (see page 11) began to relax government control over religion as part of his policy of *perestroika* (reconstruction). In 1988 he met Patriarch Pimen, head of the Church, and together they agreed to reopen many churches. Then in 1990 a new law was passed that allowed Russians to follow their religion freely.

Restoration plans

Regular services now take place at about 150 Moscow churches. Kazan Cathedral, demolished by Josef Stalin in 1936, has been rebuilt on its original site in Red Square. It reopened in 1993. The reconstruction of the Cathedral of Christ the Saviour, blown up by Stalin in 1931, was completed in 1998 (see pages 42-43). The total cost was probably more than £200 million.

Prayers are recited ➤ five times every day at Moscow Cathedral Mosque. The main service of the week is on Friday afternoon.

Moscow mosque

About 75 per cent of Russians are Christians. Muslims form the second largest religious group in the country – there are about 19 million – but most live outside Moscow in republics such as Tatarstan. The main place of worship for Moscow Muslims is the Cathedral Mosque. There is also an Islamic Centre and the Moscow Muftiyat, a religious organization that governs Moscow and many surrounding regions.

NEW RELIGIONS

The 1990 law that allowed Russians freedom of religion also allowed Bibles and other religious literature to be brought into the country once more. It also became easier for foreigners to visit. As a result, many new religious groups have arrived in Moscow. These include members of the Hare Krishna sect of Hinduism, as well as **Scientologists**. There were already about 2 million Protestant Christians in Russia, but many more have arrived from other countries hoping to attract people to join their particular group.

Jews take part in a service for ▼ the important festival of Passover at one of Moscow's synagogues.

City synagogues

There are now about 200,000 Jews in Moscow. Their numbers have been falling for years because many have emigrated to Israel and elsewhere – about 300,000 Jews left the country between 1989 and 1990. Moscow synagogues include the Choral Synagogue, which is the largest in the city. Some Muscovites have strong anti-Jewish feelings, and a synagogue was recently burned down.

INDUSTRY AND FINANCE

Russian industry first prospered during the reign of Peter the Great (1689–1725). More than 30 factories were built in Moscow, mostly textile mills producing goods such as army uniforms. Industry continued to grow over the years, providing thousands of jobs.

Communist industry

After the 1917 **revolution**, the **Communist** government took over the country's industry. It planned to turn Russia into an industrial giant. Engineering, car and metal-working industries were developed in Moscow. For years the city's largest factory was the Likhachov Motor Works, which made ZiL limousines for Communist leaders. Steel, oil and chemical industries were important too.

КОМСОМОЛ-УДАРНАЯ БРИГАДА ПЯТИЛЕТКИ.

Stalin invented **Five Year Plans** to ▲ improve industry. Posters like this, which shows a 1930s steel factory, encouraged people to work hard for their country.

▼ As Moscow industry grew, the pollution it produced was not controlled. Poisonous fumes still waft over the city today.

Industry today

Many people in modern Moscow still work in the heavy industries of the Communist era, as well as in industries such as printing and electronic engineering. Moscow is Russia's largest manufacturer of industrial goods, and produces almost a sixth of the country's total.

 Women at work in a Moscow computer factory. More than half of the city's workforce is female.

Economic change

The collapse of Communism has led to major changes in Moscow industry. Many companies have gone bankrupt because they no longer receive money from the state. Many others have been **privatized**. Thousands of people have lost their jobs. Others work only a few days each week. Wages have also fallen, and some people receive no pay at all for months.

Financial crisis

Russia's new economic system has also led to high **inflation**. As the value of the rouble plunged, prices soared. In 1998 the country's financial crisis worsened and the International Monetary Fund, an organization that helps major nations to control their currency, stepped in to help.

MONEY AND MARKETS

After Communism ended in Russia, private banks opened for the first time. By the end of 1997 there were about 1,700, and the most important are in Moscow. Russia's first post-Communist **stock market** opened in Moscow in 1991. Many Russian shares have fallen in value because the country's industries are performing so badly. When economic crisis hit Russia in 1998, the value of the rouble fell drastically, and people hurriedly withdrew their money from banks. Most stock market trading stopped.

CRIME AND PUNISHMENT

⭐ Since the fall of Communism, some crimes have increased sharply in Moscow, particularly muggings and **Mafia** violence. The government is working hard to combat these threats.

'Iron Felix' Dzerzhinsky was ▼ the USSR's first secret police chief. His huge statue stood in Moscow until 1991, when Muscovites pulled it down.

The secret police force

In the **Communist** era, the ordinary police, known as the *Militsiya*, dealt with everyday crimes such as theft. But in 1917, Lenin also set up a secret police force, called the Cheka, which caught and punished people who did not support the government. The secret police force changed its name several times, finally becoming the **KGB** in 1954. Now the KGB has been replaced by the Federal Counter-Intelligence Service.

Modern Moscow police

Today, the *Militsiya* still police Moscow. They work with the Counter-Intelligence Service to track down serious villains. They also keep order on the streets, by arresting drunks for example. In 1989 Mikhail Gorbachev set up an extra force called **OMON**. They often provide crowd control, for example at football matches.

◄ Male and female *Militsiya* officers wear a dark blue uniform, complete with a hat. Many are armed.

A police officer wearing military-style clothing uses a sniffer dog to search for drugs at a street market. ➤

Theft

Small-scale crime is common in Moscow. Bands of thieves, many of them **Gypsies**, often steal money and jewellery from pedestrians. Wealthy, well-dressed business people are particularly at risk.

THE LUBYANKA

In March 1918 the Cheka set up its headquarters in a Moscow building on Lubyanka Square. The building (below) became known as the Lubyanka.

In the 1930s the Communist leader Josef Stalin ordered the secret police to arrest millions of people who did not support the government. Many of these people were imprisoned in the Lubyanka, then tortured and shot.

Mafia mobs

Large-scale, organized crime is increasing in Moscow. Mafia gangs take over companies and use them as a cover for illegal activities such as arms-dealing. The largest Moscow Mafia mob is Solntsevskaya. It has 1,500 or more members, led by Sergei Mikhailov. Rival gang members kill one another in the streets, often using car bombs. In 1997 there were about 1,450 murders in Moscow, many of them Mafia-related.

Drug problems

Since the mid-1990s the Mafia has also been importing dangerous drugs. Addiction to these drugs is a growing problem in Moscow. In 1998 a new law was introduced that gave police greater powers to test suspected drug-takers. Conviction for smuggling or taking hard drugs can lead to the death penalty.

GETTING AROUND

The Moskva River winds through central Moscow for about 80 km and provides a quick route across the city. The Volga-Don and other canals link the river to the Baltic, Caspian and White Seas, as well as the Black Sea and its small neighbour the Sea of Azov. Cargo ships sail along this network to both inland and coastal ports.

◄ Boats travel along the Moskva River, with the Bell Tower of Ivan the Great and other splendid Kremlin buildings in the background.

River rides

People use the river to get around, especially in the summer. Tourists can take a leisurely ride on a river boat or speed along on one of the *Raketa* (rocket) hydrofoils. Long-distance travellers can also journey by boat, embarking at either the Northern or Southern River Terminal.

THE MAGNIFICENT METRO

The first Moscow Metro station opened in 1935, as part of Stalin's plan for the reconstruction of the city (see page 15). Now there are over 150

stations, and about eight million people use them each day. Unlike the grimy undergrounds of many cities, the Moscow network is clean, efficient, cheap – and beautiful. Stations such as Komsomolskaya (left), even have marble ceilings and huge crystal chandeliers.

The imposing building of Yaroslavsky ➤ Vokzal (right) was designed by the famous architect Fyodor Shekhtel (see page 41).

Roaming by rail

Moscow has nine railway stations. The first to open was St Petersburg Vokzal (station) in 1851. Today, Red Arrow express trains cover the 650 km to St Petersburg in just five hours. Trans-Siberian Railway trains depart from Yaroslavsky Vokzal, then travel across Russia to Vladivostok. Some passengers continue on branch lines to Mongolia or China.

▲ A tram rattles around Moscow. Many of the city's trams are old and delays are common. It is no fun waiting on the capital's icy streets in winter.

Cars, buses and trams

Many people travel by car, and Moscow's roads can be very busy. There are also many buses, trams and **trolley buses** which carry thousands of Muscovites around from six in the morning (five-thirty for trams) until one o'clock at night. Passengers buy tickets in advance from a kiosk or direct from the driver, and insert the tickets into a machine for punching. Inspectors check for cheats and fine anyone without a punched ticket.

Air travel

Moscow has four airports. The largest, Sheremetyevo II, is for international flights. It is situated about 32 km from the city centre, so taxis and special tourist buses bring new arrivals into the capital.

SHOPS AND MARKETS

Before the 1917 **Russian Revolution** Moscow was a shopper's paradise. Its highlight was the Upper Trading Arcade, a shopping complex that filled one side of Red Square. It had more than 1,000 shops selling goods from all over Russia and beyond. Today the building houses the famous GUM department store, which contains all kinds of shops, both Western and Russian.

Muscovites can buy a huge ▲ variety of breads from street stalls. Some are flavoured with poppy or caraway seeds.

▼ Moscow's richest citizens can afford to buy food at Yeliseyev's. Poorer people often go there too, just to stare at the mouth-watering displays.

The Temple of Gluttons

Another Moscow attraction is Yeliseyev's food store, nicknamed the Temple of Gluttons. The building was constructed in the 18th century as a princess' mansion. In the 19th century Grigory Yeliseyev bought the house. He opened a luxury grocer's there to rival the store he already owned in St Petersburg. Wealthy people flocked to the shop to buy exotic fruits, chocolates, fine wines and other delicacies. Yeliseyev's still exists and its goods are as expensive as ever.

MARKET LIFE

Many bustling markets take place in Moscow. Thousands of weekend traders gather at the market in Izmaylovskiy Park (see pages 16-17) to sell everything from **icons** to instruments such as **balalaikas** (right). Farmers bring their produce to food markets such as Cheryomushinsky market. In the past, many stalls had only a handful of poor-quality fruits or vegetables to offer. Now crops are more plentiful and stalls look much more colourful.

◄ Queuing for the few goods available in the shops became a way of life in Communist Moscow. Queues may return as Russia's economic crisis deepens.

Communist problems

Agriculture and industry did not prosper under **Communist** rule. As a result, food and other goods were in short supply, and some shops contained only empty shelves. The rouble also fell in value, so most people could not afford much.

A new start

Moscow shops have slowly come back to life since Mikhail Gorbachev's reforms. There are more stores and more goods on offer. Branches of many Western chains are about to open in a new underground shopping mall in Manezh Square, next to the Kremlin. To make shopping more pleasant, a law was passed in 1994 requiring shop assistants to be polite. But economic conditions in Russia are worsening again, and there are still serious shortages.

FOOD AND DRINK

Before the 1917 **revolution** wealthy Russians enjoyed lavish meals with many courses. These were often prepared by French chefs, many of whom came to Russia in the 18th and 19th centuries. Some set up grand restaurants in Moscow. Russian peasants, then as now, lived on simple food such as cabbage soup (*shchi*), rye bread, beetroot and potatoes, washed down with rye beer (*kvas*).

Restaurants in pre-revolutionary ▲
Moscow were among the best in the world. The rich ate there in splendour, while outside the poor went hungry.

➤ Tins of caviar, a popular Russian delicacy. The two main types are orange caviar (Siberian salmon eggs) and black caviar (sturgeon eggs).

Restaurant revival

After the revolution both dining out and home cooking took a turn for the worse. Food shortages affected rich and poor alike. Restaurants were taken over by the **state**, which led to dreary décor, slow service and badly cooked food. Even now many Russians go hungry, and there are soup kitchens on Moscow streets. But new restaurants are springing up too.

Some are **co-operatives**, where several owners put their money together to pay for premises and food.

On the menu

Many Moscow restaurants specialize in Russian food. Russian meals often begin with *zakuski*, a mixture of small dishes such as pancakes (*blini*) with caviar, gherkins, smoked herring and ham. Cabbage or beetroot soup (*borshch*) often follows, then a meat stew or joint, or perhaps fish, for example stuffed carp. *Pelmeni*, Russian-style ravioli, are another favourite, traditionally filled with pork, beef and elk. Typical desserts are ice cream or fruit pies.

Peter the Great introduced *zakuski* ▲ to Russia in the 18th century. This modern *zakuski* includes salted fish, *blinis* and caviar.

TEA AND VODKA

Russians are famous for their love of two very different drinks – tea and vodka. The **Mongols** (see page 9) first brought tea to Russia. They also introduced the samovar (below), the large urn used to heat water for the tea. Russians drink tea without milk or sugar, but usually eat something sweet with it, such as a spoonful of jam. Vodka ('little water') is a kind of alcohol made by **fermenting** grain or potatoes. It is drunk ice cold, often followed by a bite of rye bread or gherkin.

Southern specialities

Moscow also has restaurants that serve food from other regions of the former USSR, such as the southern **republics** of Armenia, Azerbaijan and Georgia. *Shashlyk* (meat kebabs) are a speciality of all three areas. One Azerbaijani dish is *piti* (lamb stew with fruit), while Georgians enjoy chicken *tsatsivi* (chicken in walnut sauce). Armenians serve *amich* (chicken with almonds and apricots).

Fast food

McDonald's arrived in Moscow in 1990 and now has three branches in the city. Since 1995 it has faced competition from a Russian fast food chain, Russkoe Bistro. Its shops sell meat pies, fish and beer.

THEATRE AND ENTERTAINMENT

Moscow has hundreds of theatres, cinemas and night clubs. Since the end of the **Communist** era, their numbers have been growing fast.

> ▲ The magnificent Bolshoi Theatre has five tiers of seating on both sides of the stalls. It can hold more than 2,000 people.

The Bolshoi Theatre

Moscow's most famous theatre is the Bolshoi (Great). It was founded by an Englishman, Michael Maddox, in 1776. The building burned down twice, and the existing theatre was constructed in 1856.

The Bolshoi Theatre has staged many ballets and operas. The first performance of Tchaikovsky's ballet *Swan Lake* took place there in 1877. In Communist times, the theatre was also used for political events, such as the ceremony to mark the USSR's foundation in 1922. Today, the Bolshoi is short of money, and new director Vladimir Vasilyev is working to improve things.

Plays

The best known theatre for drama in Moscow is the Moscow Arts Theatre (MKhAT), founded in 1898. Several plays by the important Russian dramatist Anton Chekhov were first performed there, for example *The Cherry Orchard* in 1904. MKhAT still stages serious plays, but they are no longer as popular with the public.

> A modern production at the ▲ Moscow Arts Theatre. The actors are performing a one-act comedy by Chekhov called *The Bear*.

Other theatres

A popular modern theatre is the Leninsky Komsomol Theatre, called Lenkom for short. There, director Mark Zakharov stages musicals using the latest special effects. Younger theatre-goers can visit the Central Children's Theatre and the Obraztsov Puppet Theatre, where shows are specially designed for them.

City circuses

Moscow is famous for its circuses, which include traditional acts such as performing animals, as well as clowns and acrobats. The Moscow State Circus, called the Old Circus, began in 1886. In 1971 the New Circus was set up in a 3400-seat arena in the Sparrow Hills. Tent circuses are also held at Gorky and Izmaylovskiy Parks in the summer.

CLUBS AND CASINOS

Night clubs such as the Jazz Café, and casinos such as the Sofi (right) are appearing all over Moscow. Most are so expensive that only the capital's super-rich can afford them. Some foreign business people also go there. Uniformed bouncers, many of them off-duty policemen, keep out unwanted guests. **Mafia** members, however, are often welcome – especially if they own the club.

MUSEUMS AND ART GALLERIES

Moscow has more than 80 museums and art galleries. Many are now improving their facilities to cater for growing numbers of tourists who visit the capital.

The Andrei Rublev Museum

The Andrei Rublev Museum of Early Russian Art is in the Andronikov Monastery. Andrei Rublev was a monk at the monastery in the early 15th century. He was a skilled **icon**-painter and some of his works are in the Cathedral of the Annunciation (see pages 14-15). The museum opened in 1960 and has many icons and embroideries. People also visit the site to see the monastery buildings, particularly the Cathedral of the Saviour.

The Tretyakov Gallery

Moscow's Tretyakov Gallery was founded by Pavel Tretyakov, a merchant. He began to collect paintings in 1856 and kept them in his mansion. Later he extended his house and opened it to the public. It has now been extended further and contains over 50,000 paintings, from ancient icons to the works of more recent artists such as Valentin Serov.

▲ Andrei Rublev painted this icon, *The Old Testament Trinity*, at the Andronikov Monastery. It hangs in the Tretyakov Gallery.

◄ This picture, *Girl with Peaches* by Valentin Serov, is also in the Tretyakov. It shows the daughter of a wealthy Moscow industrialist, Savva Mamontov.

Visitors to Tolstoy's house can view 16 ➤
rooms, including his study (right), where
some of his manuscripts are displayed.

The Pushkin Museum of Fine Arts

The Pushkin Museum was founded in 1887 and
contains more than 500,000 works. These include
Egyptian mummy paintings, Greek vases, Roman
statues and a world-class collection of European
paintings by artists such as Botticelli, Rembrandt
and Monet. It also holds many works taken from
Germany when the USSR occupied the country
after the Second World War.

TEKHNOPARK

In 1939 Stalin organized a show in Moscow to celebrate the
achievements of **Communist** farming. In 1959, this became
a permanent exhibition on a 220-hectare site. It was called the
USSR Economic Achievements Exhibition, or VDNKh, and had
displays on everything from industry to space travel (below).
Since the fall of Communism, the Russian government has
renamed the site Tekhnopark. Now it is
beginning to use the park to advertise
consumer goods rather than the success
of the state. One new display shows a
range of Harley-Davidson motorbikes.

House Museums

The houses of several famous
people who lived in Moscow
have been turned into museums.
The house of playwright Anton
Chekhov (see page 34) from
1886 to 1890 is now a museum.
Inside, the house looks as it did
in Chekhov's time and visitors
can see first editions of his plays.

The Russian novelist Leo Tolstoy
spent every winter from 1882 to
1901 in what is now the Tolstoy
House Museum. There he wrote
the novel *Resurrection* (1900).

The Armoury Palace

The Armoury Palace in the Kremlin
is the oldest museum in Russia –
it probably dates from the 14th
century. Now it contains the
magnificent treasures of the **tsars**,
such as jewels, crowns, robes and
Catherine the Great's wedding
and coronation dresses.

SPECIAL EVENTS

 Special events take place all year round in Moscow. Some are serious religious or political occasions, others are festivals designed to be fun for everyone.

The Winter Festival

Moscow's Winter Festival is from 25 December until 5 January. It consists of many events such as parties and concerts. New Year's Day is the highlight. Parents dress as Grandfather Frost or the Snow Maiden to give their children presents.

THE MOSCOW OLYMPICS

In 1980 the Olympic Games were held in Moscow (below). A huge, 40m-high sports complex was built for the occasion. Its stadium can hold 40,000 people and is now used for major football, rugby, ice skating and athletics competitions.

▲ Women dressed as Snow Maidens dance at a special Christmas show for children in Moscow.

Christmas

Christmas takes place on 7 January for Russian **Orthodox Christians**. Celebrations were banned in the **Communist** era, but since 1992 have been allowed again. Christians pack Moscow's churches on 6 January and stay overnight at candlelit ceremonies.

Ice festivals

In February, ice sculpture festivals are held in Gorky Park (see page 16) and elsewhere in the capital. Some people, nicknamed *morzh* (walruses), even break holes in the frozen lake to go swimming.

In the spring

Orthodox Easter occurs in March or April. Muscovites celebrate with special foods such as *kulich*, a yeast cake with almonds and raisins, and *paskha*, a spiced curd cheese cake.

In Communist times a grand military parade was held in Red Square on **May Day** (1 May). This day is still a holiday. Victory Day (9 May) marks Germany's defeat in the Second World War.

Summer fun

A new Moscow summer celebration is growing in importance, commemorating the day when Russia split away from the USSR – 12 June 1991. It is known as Independence Day and has become a public holiday. Many festivities take place in Red Square and elsewhere. Another summer event is the two-yearly Moscow Film Festival in July.

▲ Moscow's own festival, the Day of the City, takes place on 31 August each year. Many Muscovites dress up to join in its lively and colourful parades.

Autumn celebrations

Every September, the Moscow marathon is run. It begins and ends in Gorky Park. A military procession used to march across Red Square on 7 November every year to commemorate the 1917 **revolution**. Only a few people still mark the occasion. They stage small marches or take flowers to the Lenin Mausoleum.

◄ This old-style military parade took place in Moscow in November 1982. The placard on the left shows Leonid Brezhnev, who was the ruler of the USSR at the time. He died just three days later.

Moscow has been home to a variety of powerful people through the ages. Some shaped its lands and buildings, others its ways of life and thought.

Ivan the Great

Ivan the Great (Ivan III) ruled Moscow from 1462 to 1505. He was tall and handsome, and loved to laugh, eat and drink. But he was also a skilful politician who made Moscow and the surrounding state of Muscovy a great power. During his reign he conquered rival **principalities**, freed Muscovy from the **Mongols** and increased his own authority. In this way, he laid the foundations for Moscow's lasting importance and the **tsars'** immense power.

▲ Ivan the Great built two palaces in the Kremlin. The Palace of Facets contained his throne room, and the Terem Palace was his family home.

▲ Pushkin, shown here in his late 20s, was Russia's greatest poet.

Alexander Pushkin

Pushkin was born in Moscow in 1799. He became a writer and was sent away from the city in 1820 because the government disagreed with the political ideas in his poetry. In **exile**, Pushkin wrote the play *Boris Godunov* (1823) and began his verse novel *Eugene Onegin* (1823-31). Pushkin was allowed to return to Moscow in 1826, but the police followed him everywhere. Their records still exist, and show that Pushkin lived the high life at literary **salons** and clubs. He died in a duel in 1837. Moscow now has a museum dedicated to his life and work.

Osip Bove

Osip Bove was an architect who redesigned Red Square after the 1812 fire (see page 10). He also created about 500 new buildings. These included the Triumphal Arch to commemorate Russia's victory over Napoleon, and the Church of the Great Ascension, where Pushkin was married.

 Shekhtel's Gorky House Museum was originally built as a house in 1900. The outside is decorated with ironwork.

▲ Mikhail Gorbachev and his wife Raisa, who works with him for the Gorbachev Foundation.

Fyodor Shekhtel

Fyodor Shekhtel is another famous Russian architect. He designed many Moscow houses in the **Art Nouveau** style. The best example is the Gorky House Museum, which contains flower-patterned mosaics, colourful stained glass and a swirling marble staircase.

Mikhail Gorbachev

Gorbachev studied law at Moscow University and graduated in 1955. Thirty years later he became President of the USSR and introduced the reforms that brought the country to an end in 1991 (see page 11). Now he spends time working for the Moscow-based Gorbachev Foundation. It raises money for businesses and people, including victims of the Chernobyl nuclear reactor explosion in 1986.

VALENTINA TERESHKOVA

In 1963 Valentina Tereshkova (below) became the first woman in space. In 1994 she took on another high-profile role as head of the Moscow-based Russian Centre for International Scientific and Cultural

Co-operation. Her job is to build links between scientists in Moscow and those in other countries. She also organizes scholarships for science students who want to study at Russian universities.

MOSCOW'S FUTURE

Moscow has changed enormously since the end of the **Communist** era. People can vote freely, buy a wider range of goods, even make their fortunes by setting up in business. But there are likely to be problems ahead for the city.

Mighty Moscow

Moscow has managed better than the country as a whole since 1991. On average, its citizens earn much more than other Russians. Private companies have moved in, allowing the city to fund projects such as the Manezh shopping mall (see page 31). Government and business leaders have great plans for the future.

◄ The original Cathedral of Christ the Saviour took 43 years to build. The new version was completed in just three years. It is now the pride of the city.

Building projects

Offices and shops are springing up all over Moscow. The Moscow International Business Centre (MIBC), which should be complete by 2001, will contain both. It will also have a 350-room hotel and a **monorail** link to Sheremetyevo II airport. Private companies are building American-style housing estates in Moscow suburbs such as Rosinka and Pokrovsky Hills. But these are only for the very rich – the yearly rent on a Rosinka house is more than ten times the average Russian salary.

WONDER ISLAND

Moscow city government is teaming up with a Canadian company to build a theme park in the west of the capital. It will be called Wonder Island and will have a huge variety of rides on its 300-hectare site. At the moment it exists only as a model (left).

Ostankino television ▼ tower is Moscow's tallest building. The city's own television channel, Center TV, began in 1997 and is beamed from this 540 metre-high transmitter.

Bulk buying

Moscow's first hypermarket opened in the late 1990s. Ramstore, in the west of the city, sells everything from pineapples to refrigerators, and you can grab a burger while you are there too. Enka, the Turkish company that owns the store, plans four more in the capital by 1999.

Facing the future

The future for Moscow could be bright, with many new projects to revitalize the city. But the Russian economy is in crisis, thousands of Muscovites struggle to pay for food and shelter, and crime levels are rising. There is political instability, as individuals and parties struggle for power. Both citizens and city government face many challenges in the years to come.

◄ New Moscow suburbs such as Rosinka are not popular with Russians, even the most wealthy. Many people who live there are foreigners.

TIMELINE

 This timeline shows some of the most important dates in Moscow's history. All the events are mentioned earlier in this book.

9TH CENTURY AD

State of Kievan Rus established

12TH CENTURY

1147
First known record of the name Moscow, taken as date of city's foundation
1156
Prince Yury Dolgorukiy builds first Kremlin

13TH CENTURY

1237
Mongols *attack Moscow*
1263
Principality *of Muscovy established*

14TH CENTURY

1380
Russians defeat Mongols at Battle of Kulikovo Field

15TH CENTURY

1462-1505
Reign of Ivan III (the Great)
1480
Ivan III ends tribute payments to Mongols

16TH CENTURY

1533-84
Reign of Ivan IV (the Terrible)

17TH CENTURY

1605-13
*Rival **tsars** fight in Moscow*
1613
*Romanov **dynasty** comes to power*
1689-1725
Reign of Peter the Great

18TH CENTURY

1712
St Petersburg becomes Russia's capital
1755
Moscow University founded
1762-96
Reign of Catherine the Great
1771
Plague kills more than 57,000 in Moscow
1776
Bolshoi Theatre founded

19TH CENTURY

1812
French and Russian troops fight Battle
of Borodino on Moscow's outskirts

1851
First railway station, St Petersburg Vokzal,
opens

1864
Moscow Zoopark opens

1866
Moscow Conservatory founded

1873
Tretyakov Gallery opens

1877
Premiere of Tchaikovsky's Swan Lake
at Bolshoi Theatre

1886
Moscow State Circus opens

1887
Pushkin Museum of Fine Arts opens

1898
Moscow Arts Theatre (MKhAT) founded

20TH CENTURY

1905
Revolution breaks out in St Petersburg
and spreads to Moscow

1917
The Russian Revolution begins. Tsars'
rule ends and a **Communist** government
is set up under Vladimir Lenin
Cheka secret police formed

1922
Union of Soviet Socialist Republics
(USSR) formed

1928
Gorky Park opens

1928-53
Rule of Josef Stalin

1928-32
First Five Year Plan

1931
Cathedral of Christ the Saviour demolished

1935
First Moscow Metro station opens

1936
Kazan Cathedral demolished

1941
German troops invade USSR
but are driven back from Moscow

1945-1990
Cold War

1954
KGB formed

1958-64
Rule of Nikita Khrushchev

1960
Andrei Rublev Museum opens

1963
New town of Zelenograd founded

1977-82
Rule of Leonid Brezhnev

1980
Olympic Games held in Moscow

1985
Mikhail Gorbachev becomes leader
of USSR

1989
OMON security force set up

1990
New law allows freedom of religion
First McDonald's opens in Moscow

1991
Coup against Gorbachev leads to
collapse of USSR and formation
of Russian Federation

1993
Coup against Boris Yeltsin defeated
New Kazan Cathedral opens

1997
Moscow celebrates 850th anniversary

1998
Economic and political crisis hits Russia
New Cathedral of Christ the Saviour opens
New anti-drug laws introduced

GLOSSARY

Art Nouveau   A style of art and architecture that was popular from about 1890 to 1910. It featured swirling shapes and images of natural objects such as plants and leaves.

balalaika   A three-stringed instrument, usually with a triangular body.

Byzantine Empire   The empire founded by the Roman emperor Constantine when he left Rome in 330 AD. It was based in the old Greek city of Byzantium, which he renamed Constantinople after himself.

capitalist   Relating to capitalism, a system in which businesses are owned by private individuals rather than the state. *Compare Communist.*

Cold War   The time when the USSR and other Communist countries were enemies of the USA and other capitalist countries, but did not fight them in a violent 'hot' war. The Cold War lasted from about 1945 to 1990.

Communist   Relating to Communism, a system in which businesses are owned by the state and there is only one political party. *Compare capitalist.*

co-operative   A business that is owned and funded by a group of people, who share its profits.

coup   An attack designed to overthrow a ruler or government.

Cyrillic alphabet   An alphabet based on Greek letters that is used to write Russian. It is named after a 9th-century saint called Cyril, who may have invented it.

democratic   Involving all the people, especially by allowing them to elect the politicians who govern them.

dynasty   A family that rules a country for generations.

embalmed   Treated with chemicals to prevent decay.

emblem   An image that symbolizes something, for example a country.

exile   Absence from one's usual home, normally as a result of being forced to leave.

federal   Relating to a kind of government in which regional and national authorities share power.

ferment   To cause a chemical reaction that produces alcohol in foods such as potatoes. This is usually done by adding yeast.

Five Year Plans   A series of plans for economic development in the USSR. The first, introduced by Stalin, lasted from 1928 to 1932.

Greenwich Mean Time   The time in Greenwich, England, which stands on the zero line of longitude. It is used as a base for calculating the time in the rest of the world.

Gypsies   A nomadic (travelling) people who live in many countries, particularly in Europe. Gypsies originally came from India.

icon   A religious painting. Many icons are painted on wood and decorated with gold.

inflation   A continual increase in the price of goods.

KGB   The secret police of the USSR from 1954 to 1991. The initials stand for Russian words that mean 'Committee of State Security'.

Mafia   A secret criminal organization.

May Day   A holiday in honour of work and workers that is held on the first day of May.

merchant   A trader who buys and sells goods to make money.

Mongols   A warlike people who conquered Central Asia in the 13th century AD, led by Genghis Khan.

monorail   A single-track railway that is usually raised above the ground.

nationalist   A person who is loyal to and proud of his or her country, sometimes in an extreme way.

OMON   A special police force that deals with problems such as street disturbances and demonstrations. The initials stand for Russian words that mean 'workers' police support detachments'.

Orthodox Christianity   The beliefs and practices of the Orthodox churches of the East, which split from the Roman Catholic Church of the West in the 11th century AD.

Orthodox Christians   Followers of Orthodox Christianity. *See above.*

prefabricated   Ready-made. Tower blocks are often built with concrete blocks made in a factory and put together on a building site.

principality   An area of land ruled by a prince.

privatized   Sold to private owners.

republic   A country or other political unit with elected rulers and no king or queen.

revolution   A period of unrest and violence during which a government or ruling class is removed from power.

Roman Empire   The vast empire ruled from Rome from 27 BC to 476 AD. At its largest, it stretched from Britain to the Caspian Sea.

Russian Revolution   The revolution that took place in Russia in 1917. In the February Revolution, the rule of the tsars ended and a Provisional Government was set up. In the October Revolution, the government was overthrown and Communist rule under Vladimir Lenin began.

salon   A meeting of rich, fashionable guests to discuss subjects such as art and literature.

Scientologist   A member of a religion founded in California in 1954. Its members receive therapy to help them deal with bad experiences from the past. They also believe in reincarnation.

Soviet   Of or relating to the USSR, which was also known as the Soviet Union.

state   A country or other political unit that governs itself and makes its own laws.

stock market   A place where traders buy and sell company shares to make money.

tenement   A large housing block divided into flats.

tribute   Payment in money, goods or even people made by one state to another, more powerful state.

trolley buses   Buses that receive power from overhead wires like trams, but which travel on the road, not on special tram rails.

tsar   The title of the emperors of Russia. It is a form of the word 'Caesar', which was the title of the emperors of Rome.

INDEX